PITTSBURGH

VIEWS BETWEEN THE RIVERS

Photography by: Joel B. Levinson & Norman W. Schumm
and others
Introduction by: Robert Gangewere

Published by: J. B. Jeffers Ltd.
5854 Solway Street
Pittsburgh, PA 15217

Library of Congress Catalog: Card numbers 90-091954

Printed in Hong Kong by Everbest Printing Co., Ltd. through Four Colour Imports, Ltd., Louisville, Kentucky

PITTSBURGH
VIEWS BETWEEN THE RIVERS

By Robert Gangewere

Pittsburgh is a city with a story to tell, and photographers, artists, and travelers see that immediately. Visually exciting, Pittsburgh had a dramatic colonial history, a heroic part in the American Industrial Age, and after World War II, an amazing "renaissance" transformed this smoky milltown to a city constantly admired for the high quality of its urban life.

Arriving at Pittsburgh from the West, the traveler comes through the Fort Pitt Tunnel and is suddenly confronted by a cityscape that leaps to the eye. "It is the only city in America with an entrance," says *The New York Times*.

Apparent at a glance is Pittsburgh's reason for existence—the three rivers which made it a transportation hub in the mountains of western Pennsylvania. In the 18th century it was the Gateway to the West, since the Ohio River flows 980 miles to the Mississippi and then south to the Gulf of Mexico, or north to the Missouri and Northwest.

The Iron City of the early 19th century became the Steel City of the post Civil War era and the 20th century. Pittsburgh's many bridges reveal a history of engineering and design, and its many hills and valleys contain stories of ethnic populations. The modern city, erected on the site of the world's most famous milltown, tells a story of partnership between government and private business in redirecting the city's economic energy and literally changing the look of a city.

The Pittsburgh experience for the visitor, however brief, has several levels. First there is the surprise of "the Arrival": the view of the city as one emerges from the Fort Pitt Tunnel never fails to please. Then there is **the City** itself, highly concentrated placement of 19th century buildings next to post-modern architecture in a reasonable, easily grasped way. Next there are **the Neighborhoods,** marked by Old World churches and ethnic stability, with a strong sense of place.

Then there is the second city, the university town—**Oakland,** with its museums, educational and medical facilities, and pleasurable parklands. These complexes are shaping Pittsburgh for the 21st century. Then there are the **Pleasures of the City** urbane and familial, from the Symphony to the Zoo, from the Art Festival to the Regatta, from sculling on the river to water skiing. The city is a strong **Sports** City. Finally the **Hidden Treasures** of the city tries to convey just a few of its jewels.

In these photographs the pace and variety of Pittsburgh are felt—a city of under 400,000 residents which acts as a regional mecca for millions in the tri-state area of Pennsylvania, Ohio and West Virginia, people who relish its big city style, its real traditions and sophisticated pleasures.

3

The riverboat era lives on with the Majestic, one of the Gateway Clipper Fleet, that tours the three rivers.

Those arriving by air find the city's towers standing tall against a backdrop of Pennsylvania hills.

Travelers from the north move quickly down the East Street Valley Expressway, across the Veteran's Memorial Bridge and into the city center.

Barges laden with coal on western Pennsylvania waters have been a sign of the region's prosperity since the mid-19th century.

The Duquesne Incline (1877) is one of two remaining inclines that have survived as a form of transportation from the Mt. Washington hills into the city.

Rapid transit from the south provides efficient access to the city. On arrival this attractive commuter system proceeds underground as it makes a 1.5 mile loop through the Golden Triangle.

THE CITY

At sunrise, Pittsburgh's eastern commuters begin their daily routine with this visually exciting view.

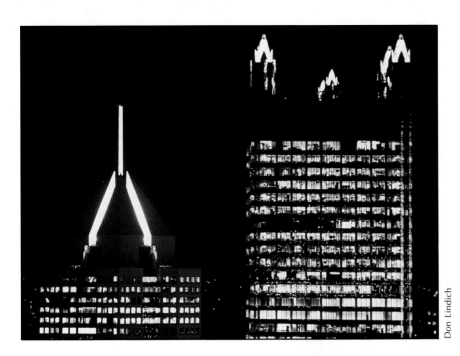

The mysterious mast of Fifth Avenue Place and the tower of PPG Place are the cities modern landmarks at night.

Don Lindich

On Oliver Ave., the city takes on an old world appearance. Here also is the symbol of its conservative tradition—the exclusive Duquesne Club.

Allegheny County Courthouse and Jail (1888), designed by Henry Hobson Richardson, is one of America's greatest 19th Century Buildings.

Trinity Episcopal Cathedral (1872) on Oliver Avenue has a historic graveyard to ponder.

Fort Pitt Block House (1764) (left) in Point State Park is the last remaining building of the old fort and the oldest structure in the city. One of the newest structures is Fifth Avenue Place (1987) (above), one of the Post-Modern towers that adorn the city. It was deliberately scaled down to keep the urban skyline interesting.

Horne's Department Store sports a giant Christmas tree every year. Also another local holiday tradition is America's first commercial radio station, KDKA's fund drive for Children's Hospital.

PPG Place (1984) by Philip Johnson and John Burgee is a castle made of glass, with a dramatic courtyard. The Wintergarden (left) is its enclosed area for displays and relaxing year round.

Saks Fifth Avenue is across the street from Mellon Square with its cascading waterfalls. This open plaza is a favorite retreat during warm weather for many that find themselves in "Town."

Equitable Plaza was created during the 1950s, when Pittsburgh demolished acres of industrial buildings during its famous Renaissance.

Mt. Washington is a popular spot for visitors to stroll and identify Downtown points of interest.

The clock at Kaufmann's, the city's largest department store, is a favorite place for shoppers to meet.

The details of Pittsburgh's older buildings, especially along Fourth Ave., are a constant source of interest to pedestrians.

Norman W. Schumm

The Strip District, just east of the Downtown, begins supplying food to city merchants early in the morning and becomes a busy food market to the shoppers as the day wears on.

The city takes on a futuristic appearance thru the early morning mist, as the Mellon Bank One, County Courthouse, Chatham Complex and the Arena appear.

Looking up the Allegheny one comes to realize why Pittsburgh has become known as the City of Bridges.

Pittsburgh's North Side, the home of the Allegheny General Hospital Complex (background), is rich with historic and cultural interests.

St. John the Baptist Ukrainian Catholic Church (1895) on Pittsburgh's South Side is just one of the Eastern European churches that give the city skyline an exotic quality.

THE NEIGHBORHOODS

Pittsburgh's unquestioned strength is in its strongly identified neighborhoods. Here homes clustered on the hill in South Side overlook Pittsburgh's "second city," Oakland.

The Church in Rankin (right), as in so many neighborhoods throughout the city, identifies the heart of the community. (Below) Immaculate Heart of Mary Church (1906) literally is at the crossroads of the Polish Hill neighborhood.

Milltown America never looked more intriguing than in the clusters of homes that crown Pittsburgh's slopes. A South Side ("Old Birmingham") scene with flats in foreground.

East Liberty, in the spreading valley east of the city, is dominated by the Presbyterian Cathedral. Motor Square Garden, an early automobile center, has recently been beautifully restored.

The Steel Mill in Hazelwood, along the Monongahela, is one of Pittsburgh's few remaining mills within the city limits.

At the entrance to the Hill District, St. Benedict the Moor opens his arms atop the tower of the church of the same name.

Troy Hill, atop the mountain immediately south of the city, has been home to generations of German Americans since the late 1800s.

The fountain at Allegheny Center on the North Side, with America's first free city supported Carnegie Library (1890) and the Buhl Science Center in the background.

The city from the north, with houses clustered along the rim of Spring Hill.

Fog over the city as viewed by residents atop Mt. Washington.

George Haeck

Buena Vista Street in the Mexican War Streets District of the North Side. This neighborhood bears the street names of famous Mexican-American War Places. Many of the homes along the streets have been restored and contain intricate facia details.

Squirrel Hill is a popular neighborhood with strong Jewish traditions and an international perspective. It is situated between the two largest city parks, adjacent to the university and medical center and an easy commute to the Golden Triangle. It is a fine area in which to live, raise a family, and shop.

On this page and the following fold out pages are the panoramic views of the city that have many people saying "Pittsburgh is America's best kept secret." The holiday season is traditionally welcomed in with "Light-Up Night." The bridges of the city are its vital arteries. The view from Mt. Washington is a familiar perspective of Pittsburgh. Oakland is a "second city" dominated by the universities, and the medical complex. Originally made possible by Pittsburgh's heavy industrial base, Oakland has developed into a national center for research and high technology in medicine and education.

Open for City Centerfold

OAKLAND

—THE UNIVERSITY, MEDICAL AND CULTURAL CENTER

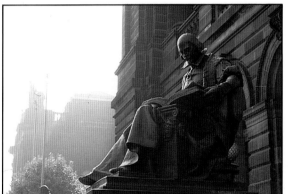

The Carnegie, a great museum and library complex founded by Andrew Carnegie in 1895, was the historic core for the cultural growth of Oakland. Outside the entrance to this palace of culture are symbolic sculptures, including one of Shakespeare.

Heinz Chapel, a non-denominational medieval chapel, is on the campus of the University of Pittsburgh, and honors the founder of the Pittsburgh food company.

The entrance to the Carnegie Museum of Art is the
Sarah Scaife Gallery, added to the Carnegie in 1974.
The Carnegie Museum of Natural History is called the
"Home of the Dinosaurs" because of its famous col-
lection of fossil dinosaurs.

Inside the Cathedral of Learning are these medieval interior arches. They become a backdrop for students to meet and study. This is also the home of Pitt's Nationality Rooms, which are reproductions of classrooms from around the world.

The Mary Schenley Memorial—"Song of Nature" at the entrance to Schenley Park with the Cathedral of Learning of the University of Pittsburgh behind it.

Mellon Institute, a 1937 applied research center for Pittsburgh Industries, joined Carnegie Mellon University in 1967.

The old and the new at CMU. Carnegie Mellon University began as the Carnegie Technical Schools with buildings like Machinery Hall (now Hamerschlag Hall) and grew into an advanced computer research center with buildings like Wean Hall to the right.

The George Westinghouse Memorial in
Schenley Park, dedicated to the Pittsburgh
inventor and industrialist.

Cross country skiing on the golf course in
Schenley Park—a major park in the heart of the
city.

Phipps Conservatory (1893) features botanical displays and flower shows.

Oakland is the home of some of the country's finest hospitals and research facilities and the hub of the city's medical activities. Within a six block radius one finds Hospitals like Magee Women's, Montefiore, Eye and Ear, Western Psychiatric, Children's, Falk Clinic, Presbyterian, as well as the University of Pittsburgh Medical and Dental Colleges.

PLEASURES OF THE CITY

Fourth of July at the Point

Water skiing and sculling on the rivers—signs that the rivers have become a major source of pleasure for everyone.

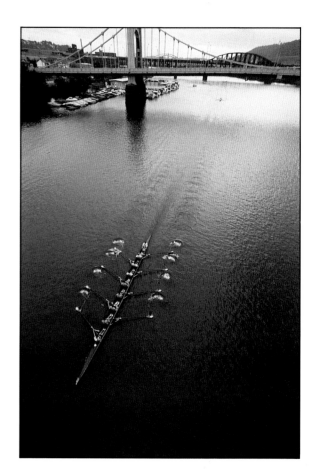

Norman W. Schumm

The Civic Arena, with its great retractable dome, opens to the setting sun for the concert goers in attendance.

Heinz Hall, first of the giant Pittsburgh movie palaces to be restored as a contemporary performance hall, and the home of the Pittsburgh Symphony Orchestra.

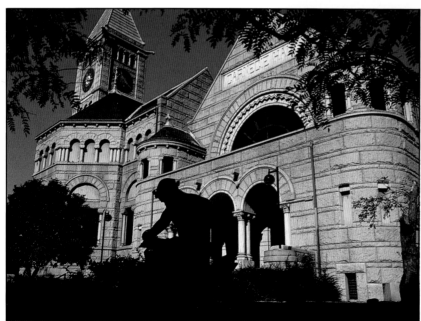

The Pittsburgh Public Theater is housed in another adapted architectural space—the 1890 Music Hall in the Allegheny Branch of the Carnegie Library of Pittsburgh.

The ballet in Benedum Center for the Performing Arts, one of two great restored theaters in Downtown Pittsburgh and one block away from Heinz Hall.

Three Rivers Art Festival Time...

Outdoor sculpture park at Allegheny Landing provides an excellent place to stroll along the Allegheny River, and view the skyline from the North. It is within a few blocks of the area that has exhibits and performances as part of the city's yearly Three Rivers Art Festival. It is a good place to start the Festival Experience.

The Three Rivers Art Festival, toward the end of the spring season, lasts for several weeks and draws a million people from Pennsylvania, Ohio and West Virginia. Colorful pavilions house the art, and there are numerous outdoor concerts and performances occurring each day throughout the Downtown area, as well as in the North and South Sides.

Three Rivers Regatta Time...

Leo Hsu

The city celebrates a festival on the rivers each summer with its annual Three Rivers Regatta. Hundreds of thousands of tri-state residents crowd the river banks and overlooks to view the Formula One Speedboat Races, anything that floats race, balloon races, the paddlewheel races, the fireworks, and all the boats that come to dock and party along the rivers.

Formula One Speedboat Races.

Kennywood Park on the banks of the Monongahela River is a spacious old style amusement park with roller coasters famous for their thrilling rides. Tops on the list is the Thunderbolt pictured here.

Leo Hsu

The traditional Pittsburgh Zoo has been modernized, featuring state-of-the-art natural environments for the animals, yet still retains some past features. The Children's Zoo provides a special area for getting close to the animals.

Station Square is a turn-of-the-century railroad station that has been strikingly transformed into a wonderful dining and shopping complex through the guidance of the Pittsburgh History and Landmarks Foundation.

SPORTS

Three Rivers Stadium, on the banks of the Ohio River and just across the river from the Golden Triangle, is one of the first things people notice as they come through the Fort Pitt Tunnels. It says to all that Pittsburgh is a sports town of major league stature. The stadium is the home of the Pittsburgh Pirates and the Pittsburgh Steelers.

Norman W. Schumm

Roberto Clemente was the famous Pittsburgh Pirate center fielder of the 1960's until he died in an airplane crash in 1972 while on a mission of mercy. Pittsburghers' love of baseball was rekindled because of Roberto's play and his contribution to the city was memorialized by naming the riverside park beside the stadium after him. (see page 68)

THE GREAT ONE—ROBERTO CLEMENTE 1934 - 1972
His Memorable Hit—Number 3000 September 30, 1972

Pirate opener, always a joyous Rite of Spring.

Tailgate parties are a Pittsburgh tradition before Pittsburgh Steeler games.

The Pittsburgh Penguins brought hockey to new heights in the 1980's. Home ice is at the Civic Arena and Mario Lemieux is sports hero to the passionate fans that fill it.

RUNNING IN PITTSBURGH

Whether you run or bike, the Pittsburgh streets and parks offer some of the most beautiful and varied routes. There are a lot of organized competitions when the joggers want to measure up to others. The Pittsburgh Marathon in the spring pits world-class runners against locals and takes place through neighborhoods that come out in the thousands to cheer everyone on. In the fall mostly local joggers try their skills against 10,000 others in the 6K Great Race that starts in Squirrel Hill and ends, as most city events do, at Point State Park.

Great Race, just after start, in Squirrel Hill.

Alan Amster

Pittsburgh Marathon, through Shadyside.

Pittsburgh Marathon, coming out of South Side heads across
the Birmingham Bridge.

Jeffrey B. Levinson

Renaissance II
—the city's building phases of 1970's and 80's.

One Oxford Center, an elegant address for your office, as well as high fashion shopping and mid-day lunches.

The PPG modern glass complex is a symbol of the start of the city's Renaissance II development during the 1970's and 80's. The Fifth Avenue Place, just behind, was the last building in the development.

CNG Tower (1988) has an unusual arched crown on top, and is in contrast to the top of the Keenan Building (1907), next door.

HIDDEN TREASURES

The city has many intriguing spots and events tucked away for city enthusiasts and visitors to explore. One such treasure is its many vistas that change constantly during the day and during the year.

The Rotunda of the 1900 Pennsylvania Railroad Station is now a Beaux Arts Entrance to an apartment complex adapted from the old station.

The Grand Concourse at Station Square, a restaurant created within the lavish foyer of the 1898 P.&L.E. Railroad Station.

The Croation Church in Millvale contains remarkable murals showing the migration of Eastern Europeans to America, the struggles of the laboring classes, and World War I.

The ''Buggy Races'' every spring allow CMU students to compete in building and racing powerless vehicles through the Campus and Schenley Park.

When Pittsburghers celebrate everyone comes...and the city shines at its best.

This is light-up night as seen from Mt. Washington.

Joel B. Levinson and Norman Schumm have each been capturing the Pittsburgh image on film for over thirty years. The two photographers are both well known locally and their photographs have been featured in many other publications.

Joel B. Levinson has had his photographs published starting back in 1953 when he was an Engineering student at Carnegie Institute of Technology (now CMU). Over the last 15 years more of his photographic work has become known throughout the area. His first book, *PITTSBURGH MOMENTS*, published by *University of Pittsburgh Press*, was done with Lynn Johnson. It was a black and white study of the city during the early 1980's. His one man show, *WOMEN AS I FIND THEM*, presented around the city in 1988, was done in photojournalist style, both black and white and color. Most of his works presented herein were taken with a NIKON FE2 or F3, using an array of lenses. You might be able to pick out those he took with his favorite 17mm Tamron lens.

The Clemente picture on page 58 shows the Pirate right fielder's memorable 3000 hit. Joel put the memorial photo together within days of Roberto's death, but it was never published until now. Needless to say it is one of Joel's most favorite and least known photographs.

Norman W. Schumm, a corporate pilot for PNC Financial Corp, has pursued photography as an avocation since high school. He is a darkroom enthusiast, working in black and white, as well as color. He has had several one man shows, the most recent featuring fifty black and white "fine art" photographs. In 1975, 1980, and again in 1988, author Stefan Lorant engaged Norman to take photographs for the updated editions of *PITTSBURGH, THE STORY OF AN AMERICAN CITY*. His pictures of Pittsburgh and original "fine art" photographs may be seen in art galleries and framing stores throughout the Pittsburgh area.

Leo Hsu, Susan L. Nega, Jeffrey B. Levinson, Alan Amster, Don Lindich, and George Haeck are all Pittsburghers. They all were at the right place at the right time and saw something worth capturing. With the exception of Leo, Susan and Don, the others consider themselves truly amateur. Leo has worked as a photographic assistant to Joel as well as Jo Leggett while he pursued his college education. Susan works as Joel's assistant now.

Bob Gangewere wrote the introduction and many of the picture captions. Like both Joel and Norm he, too, is a Pittsburgh enthusiast. He is editor of the *Carnegie Magazine,* and written many articles for trade journals and local papers.

The driving force behind the publication of this book was Joel's wife Toba, to whom this book is dedicated with everlasting love.